James Curtis Hepburn

The Old Man And tThe Devils

.

James Curtis Hepburn

The Old Man And tThe Devils

ISBN/EAN: 9783744704212

Printed in Europe, USA, Canada, Australia, Japan

Cover: Foto ©Thomas Meinert / pixelio.de

More available books at **www.hansebooks.com**

THE OLD MAN AND THE DEVILS.

JAPANESE FAIRY TALES, No 7.

瘤　取　ドクトル　ヘボン　譯

明治十九年四月二十七日版權免許同六月出版

出版人 東京府平民長谷川武次郎

東京 南佐柄木町二番地 總發賣所 弘文社

PUBLISHED BY THE KOBUNSHA

2 Minami Saegicho, TOKYO.

THE OLD MAN & THE DEVILS

long time ago there was an old man who had a big lump on the right side of his face. One day he went into the mountain

to cut wood, when the rain began to pour and the wind to blow so very hard, that finding it impossible to return home, and filled with fear, he took refuge in the hollow of an old tree. While sitting there doubled up and unable to sleep, he heard the confused sound of many voices in the distance gradually approaching to where he was. He said to himself, "how strange! I thought I was all alone in the mountain but I hear the voices of many people"; so taking courrage he peeped out, and saw a great crowd of strange looking beings. Some were red and dressed in green clothes; others were black and dressed in red clothes; some had only one eye; others had no mouth: indeed it is quite impossible to describe their varied and strange looks.

They kindled a fire,
so that it became as
light as day. They
sat down in two

cross rows,

and began to drink wine and make merry just like human beings. They passed the winecup around so often that many of them became very drunk. One of the young devils got up and began to sing a merry song and to dance; so also many others; some danced well, others badly. One said, "we have had uncommon fun to-night, but I would like to see something new". The old man losing all fear, thought he would like to dance, and saying "let come what will, if I die for it I will have a dance too", crept out of the hollow tree, and with his cap slipped over his nose and his axe sticking in his belt began to dance. The devils in great surprise jumped up saying, "Who is this"; but the old man advancing and receding, swaying to and fro, and posturing this way and that way, the whole crowd laughed and enjoyed the fun, saying, "how well the old man dances, you must always come and join us in our sport;

but for fear you might not
come you must give us a
pledge that you will".

So the devils consulted together and agreeing that the lump on his face, which was a token of wealth, was what he valued most highly, demanded that it should be taken. The old man replied,

"I have had this lump many years and would not without good reason part with it; but you may have it, or an eye or my nose either if you wish".

So the devils laid hold of it, twisting and pulling, and took it off without giving him any pain, and put it away as a pledge that he would come back. Just then the day began to dawn and the birds to sing, so the devils hurried away.

The old man felt his face and found it quite smooth and not a trace of the lump left. He forgot all about cutting wood, and hastened home. His wife seeing him, exclaimed in great surprise "what has

happened to you". So he told her
all that had befallen him.

Now among the neighbours there was another old man who had a big lump on the left side of his face. Hearing all about how

the old man had got rid of his lump, he determined that he would also try the same plan to get rid of his lump. So he went and crept into the hollow tree and waited for the devils to come. Sure enough, they came just as he was told. They sat down, drank wine and made merry just as they did before. The old man afraid and trembling crept out of the hollow tree. The devils welcomed him saying. "the old man has come, now let us see him dance" This old man was awkward and did not dance as well as the other. So the devils cried out, "You dance badly, and are getting worse and worse, we will give you back the lump which we took from you as a pledge". Upon this one of the devils brought the lump and stuck it on the other side of his face; so the old man returned home with a lump on each side of his face.